MAX AND SAM

SHORT A WORDS	SIGHT-WORDS
Word Preview	Word Preview
Max	is
lad	a
pal	has
Sam	the
cat	of
fat	in
pats	on
bag	and
cap	
sat	
mat	
ran	
nabs	
lap	
nap	

Book 1 Short A
By Miranda Burnette

Illustrations by Blueberry Illustrations

Keys to Success Publishing, LLC
Atlanta, GA

Copyright © 2016 by Miranda Burnette.

All rights reserved. Published by Keys to Success Publishing, LLC. No part of this book may be reproduced or transmitted in any form or by any means electronic, mechanical, recording, or by any information storage and retrieval system, including photocopying, without permission in writing from the author or publisher.

Printed in the U.S.A.
ISBN-13: 978-0692823507
ISBN-10: 0692823506

Keys to Success Publishing
Atlanta, GA

This book is dedicated to my four-year old grandson, Shaun Jr. Shaun Jr., you have greatness on the inside of you, and you are a champion. So keep your eyes on the prize and press on to be all God created you to be.

Max is a lad.
Max has a pal.

Sam is a cat.
Sam is a fat cat.

Sam is the pal of Max.

Max pats Sam.

Max has a cap.

Sam ran.
Max ran.

Max nabs Sam!

Sam sat on Max's lap.

READING ACTIVITIES

1. What is the boy's name in the story?

2. Name three words that rhyme with Max.

3. What is the cat's name?

4. Use the word 'cat' in a sentence.

5. Put one consonant before each 'at' and make four words that were in the story.

   ___ at   ___at   ___at   ___at

Miranda Burnette is the president and founder of Miranda Burnette Ministries, Inc., I Can Christian Academy, Inc., and Keys to Success Publishing, LLC.

She is the author of the following books: *Dare to Dream and Soar Like an Eagle*, *Success Starts in Your Mind*, *Leader to Leader*, *Winning With the Power of Love*, and *Baseball Pals*, a children's book.

Miranda is passionate about teaching. Prior to resigning and starting her own business, I Can Christian Academy, Inc. in 2009, she taught elementary school for 13 years in the public school system. She has taught several different grade levels but enjoys teaching kindergarten students. Her favorite subject to teach is reading, and she especially loves teaching preschoolers and kindergarten students how to read, as well as teaching young students how to write.

Miranda loves writing inspirational and children's books, reading, and spending time with her three grandchildren.

www.ingramcontent.com/pod-product-compliance
Lightning Source LLC
Chambersburg PA
CBHW041810040426
42449CB00001B/51